WORLD FAMOUS BUILDINGS

Petronas Towers

by Alicia Z. Klepeis

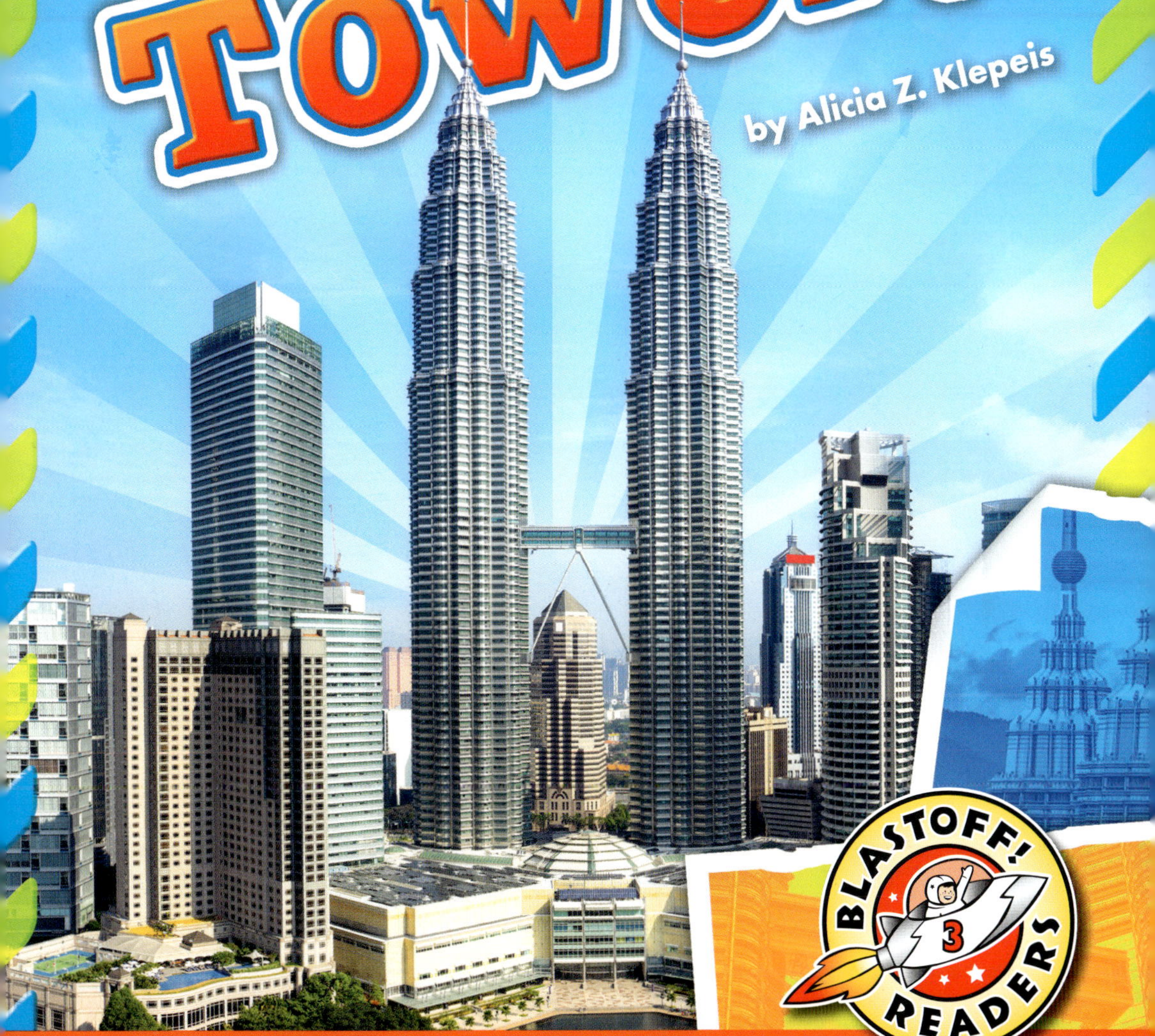

BLASTOFF! READERS, AN IMPRINT OF BELLWETHER MEDIA BY FLUTTERBEE

Blastoff! Readers are carefully developed by literacy experts to build reading stamina and move students toward fluency by combining standards-based content with developmentally appropriate text.

Level 1 provides the most support through repetition of high-frequency words, light text, predictable sentence patterns, and strong visual support.

Level 2 offers early readers a bit more challenge through varied sentences, increased text load, and text-supportive special features.

Level 3 advances early-fluent readers toward fluency through increased text load, less reliance on photos, advancing concepts, longer sentences, and more complex special features.

★ **Blastoff! Universe**

Reading Level

Blastoff! Beginners — Grade K

Blastoff! Readers — Grades 1–3

Blastoff! Discovery — Grade 4

This edition first published in 2026 by Bellwether Media, Inc.

For information regarding permission, write to Bellwether Media, Inc., Attention: Permissions Department, 3500 American Blvd W, Suite 150, Bloomington, MN 55431.

Library of Congress Cataloging-in-Publication Data is available at www.loc.gov or upon request from the publisher.

ISBN: 9798893048087 (hardcover)
ISBN: 9798893049084 (ebook)

Editor: Betsy Rathburn Designer: Laura Sowers

Printed in the United States of America, North Mankato, MN.

Table of Contents

What Are the Petronas Towers?

The Petronas Towers are a famous landmark in Malaysia. They rise above Kuala Lumpur. This is the country's capital city.

These thin skyscrapers are the world's tallest twin buildings.

The towers house many business offices. One is PETRONAS. This is Malaysia's national oil and gas company.

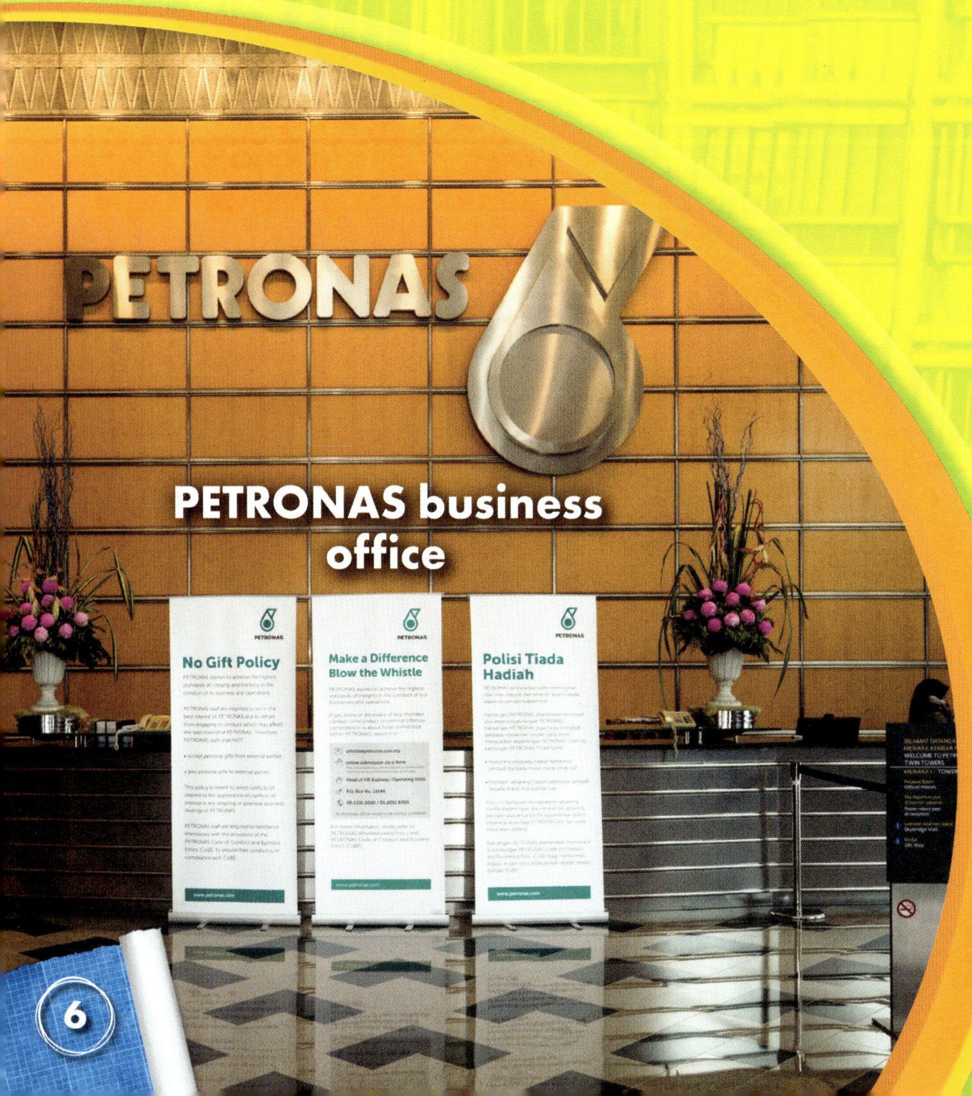

PETRONAS business office

observation deck

People visit the **observation decks** for incredible views. Prayer rooms and a concert hall are also on site.

History of the Petronas Towers

Kuala Lumpur in 1989

Kuala Lumpur grew fast in the 1980s. Leaders wanted a building to show the city's growth. They searched for an **architect** to **design** it.

They chose César Pelli. Diamonds shining in the sun **inspired** his design.

César Pelli

Construction of the towers began in 1993.

Machines drove 104 **piles** into the ground. Workers poured **concrete** to make a **raft**. This **foundation** supports the heavy towers.

foundation

The towers are made of **reinforced** concrete. Stainless steel and glass cover the outside.

Building Supplies

Shiny steel **spires** top the towers. The towers opened in 1999.

Parts of the Petronas Towers

The towers stretch 1,483 feet (452 meters) tall. They rise 88 stories. People can visit the highest observation deck on the 86th floor.

A two-story Skybridge is located at the 41st and 42nd floors.

Skybridge

Super Skybridge

What It Does	connects the towers and gives visitors a great view
How High It Is	558 feet (170 meters) above the ground

Malaysia's national religion is **Islam**. Each tower's floor plan is an eight-pointed star. This shape means **unity** and **harmony** in Islam.

Size Comparison

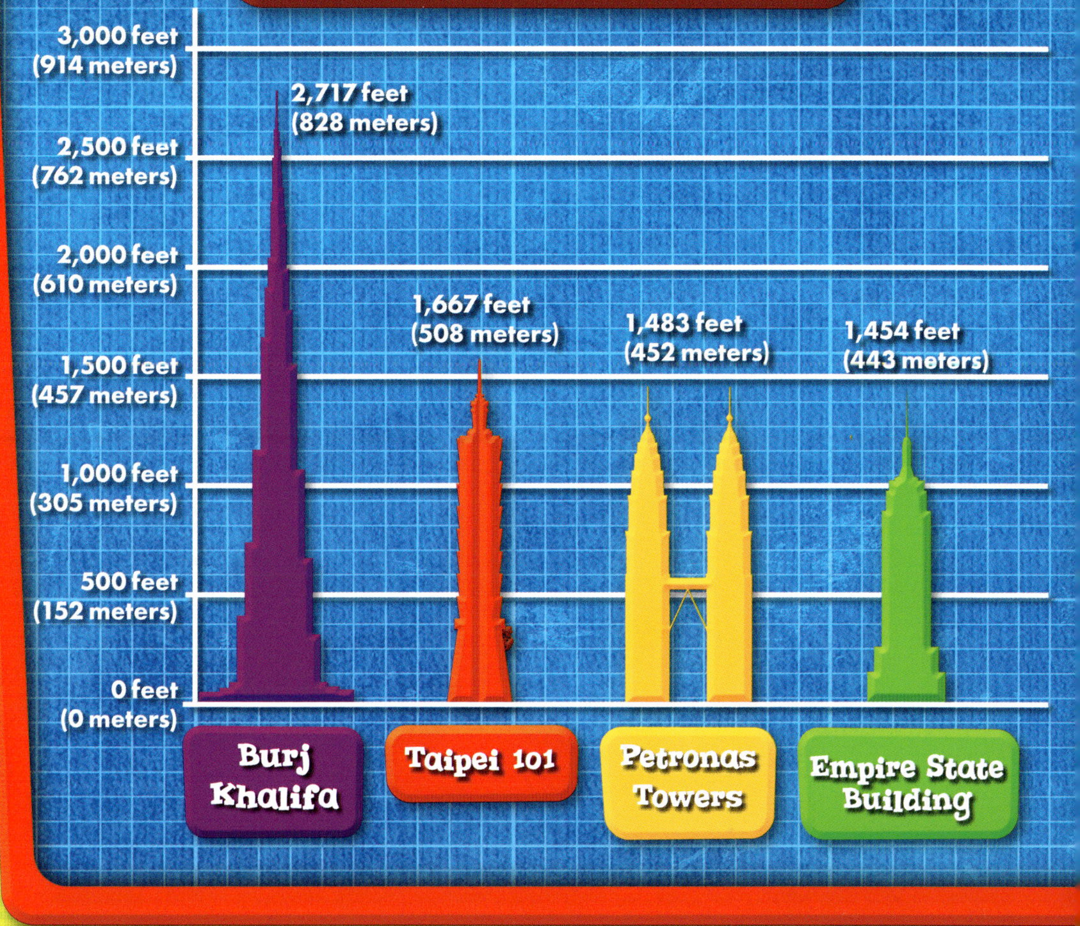

Designs inside the towers show off local crafts. These include weaving patterns and wood carvings.

The Petronas Towers Today

Many people work in the Petronas Towers. Security staff do. Shop and restaurant workers do too.

It takes workers about two months to clean all 32,000 windows!

workers cleaning windows

The towers are among Malaysia's most visited landmarks. More than one million people visit each year. They ride up in its high-speed elevators.

These towers impress anyone who visits them!

7:38
AmBank
SURIA KLCC
ISETAN

Glossary

architect—a person who designs buildings and gives advice during their construction

concrete—a hard, strong building material made with cement, sand, rocks, and water

design—to make a plan for a building, object, or pattern

foundation—the base or support on which a building rests

harmony—the state of being in agreement or at peace with others

inspired—gave someone an idea about what to do or create

Islam—a religion based on belief in Allah as the only god and in Muhammad as Allah's follower

observation decks—platforms built so that people can look out at a view

piles—heavy beams or posts driven into the ground to support the foundation of a building

raft—a layer of reinforced concrete that forms a building's foundation

reinforced—containing metal inside for added strength

spires—pointed structures at the top of a building

unity—the state of being connected with others

To Learn More

AT THE LIBRARY

Hurley, Jorey. *Skyscraper.* New York, N.Y.: Simon & Schuster Books for Young Readers, 2019.

Hynson, Colin. *Colossus: The World's Most Amazing Feats of Engineering.* Somerville, Mass.: Candlewick Press, 2021.

Klepeis, Alicia Z. *Malaysia.* Minneapolis, Minn.: Bellwether Media, 2022.

ON THE WEB

FACTSURFER

Factsurfer.com gives you a safe, fun way to find more information.

1. Go to www.factsurfer.com.
2. Enter "Petronas Towers" into the search box and click 🔍.
3. Select your book cover to see a list of related content.

Index

The images in this book are reproduced through the courtesy of: Patrick Foto, front cover, p. 3; Stockbym, front cover (inset 1); HU Art and Photography, front cover (inset 2), p. 15; Mariana Ianovska, pp. 4-5; CEphoto, Uwe Aranas/ Wikipedia, p. 6; Magic Orb Studio, pp. 6-7; David Cooper/ Alamy Stock Photo, pp. 8-9; Jon LC, p. 9; Presidencia de la N. Argentina/ Wikipedia, p. 9 (César Pelli); UPALI ATURUGIRI/ Contributor/ Getty Images, p. 10; Construction Photography/ Avalon/ Contributor/ Getty Images, pp. 10-11; Arafah_photography, p. 12; Juhku, p. 13 (concrete); AlexRosu, p. 13 (stainless steel); Alpar, p. 13 (glass); MartiBstock, p. 13; Kevin Lang/ Alamy Stock Photo, p. 14; MOHD RASFAN/ Contributor/ Getty Images, pp. 14-15; tobiasjo, p. 16; Joshua Davenport, pp. 18-19; TENGKU BAHAR/ Stringer/ Getty Images, p. 19; josewsy, p. 20; Neil Bussey, pp. 20-21; evannovostro, p. 23.